# A Look at
## at
# EROSION
# AND
# WEATHERING

Cecelia H. Brannon

**Enslow Publishing**
101 W. 23rd Street
Suite 240
New York, NY 10011
USA

enslow.com

Published in 2016 by Enslow Publishing, LLC
101 W. 23rd Street, Suite 240, New York, NY 10011

**Library of Congress Cataloging-in-Publication Data**
Brannon, Cecelia H., author.
A look at erosion and weathering / Cecelia H. Brannon.
    pages cm. – (The rock cycle)
Audience: Ages 8+
Audience: Grades 4 to 6.
Summary: "Describes weathering and erosion in terms of Earth's rock cycle"—Provided by publisher.
Includes bibliographical references and index.
ISBN 978-0-7660-7280-0 (library binding)
ISBN 978-0-7660-7278-7 (pbk.)
ISBN 978-0-7660-7279-4 (6-pack)
1.  Erosion—Juvenile literature. 2.  Weathering—Juvenile literature. 3.  Geochemical cycles—Juvenile literature.
I. Title.
 QE571.B76 2016
 551.3'52—dc23
                    2015029177

Printed in the United States of America

**To Our Readers:** We have done our best to make sure all websites in this book were active and appropriate when we went to press. However, the author and the publisher have no control over and assume no liability for the material available on those websites or any websites they may link to. Any comments or suggestions can be sent by e-mail to customerservice@enslow.com.

**Photo Credits:** Throughout book: Plus69/Shutterstock.com (sand erosion texture), Chaikom/Shutterstock.com (cracked red earth borders), New Saetiew/Shutterstock.com (dry gray soil borders), Christine Yarusi (series logo, four-rock dingbat), Pixeljoy/Shutterstock.com (eroded rock texture in chapter headers); cover, p. 1 OliverSved/Shutterstock.com (dry brown soil, left), black-board1965/Shutterstock.com (red soil erosion, center), oksmit/Shutterstock.com (beach ero-sion, right); p. 4 ZoranKrstic/Shutterstock.com; p. 7 Johan Swanepoel/Shutterstock.com; p. 8 ZeWrestler/Wikimedia Commons/Rockcycle2.jpg/public domain; p. 9 kojihira-no/Shutterstock.com; p. 10 Phil MacD Photography/Shutterstock.com; p. 11 Richard A McMil-lin/Shutterstock.com (top), Bildagentur Zoonar GmbH/Shutterstock.com; p. 12 Zacarias Perei-era de Mata/Shutterstock.com; p. 13 Alexandr Makarov/Shutterstock.com (top), Daderot/Wikimedia Commons/ Bixi_stele_(wrapped),_Harvard_University,_Cambridge,_MA_-_IMG_4607.JPG/public do-main (bottom); p. 14 DEA/N. CIRANI/De Agostini/Getty Images; p. 15 Patrick Fo-to/Shutterstock.com; p. 16 gkuna/Shutterstock.com; p. 17 Jerry Lin/Shutterstock.com; p. 18 Tupungato/Shutterstock.com; p. 20 Yuri Kravchenko/Shutterstock.com (top), gra-cious_tiger/Shutterstock.com (bottom); p.21 Barna Tanko/Shutterstock.com; p. 22 Josef Hanus/Shutterstock.com (top), Ursula Perreten/Shutterstock.com (bottom); p. 23 © iStockpho-to.com/MartinKovalenkov; p. 24 Denis Kichatof/Shutterstock.com; p. 25 Andrew Kotura-nov/Shutterstock.com; p. 26 Dan Schreiber/Shutterstock.com (top), © iStockpho-to.com/ficklefable (bottom); p. 27 robbinsbox/Shutterstock.com; p. 29 wizda-ta/Shutterstock.com.

# Contents

Ice is a common cause
of weathering.

# What Are
# EROSION AND
# WEATHERING?

Rocks are strong, but water and wind can be stronger. These forces can break down rocks through the processes of **weathering** and **erosion**.

## Breaking Down and Moving

Weathering is the process by which surface rocks, soil, and minerals break down into smaller pieces. Many things can cause weathering, including water, wind, ice, and climate change. For example, when ice gets inside a crack in a rock, it can break pieces off the rock, which weathers it.

Erosion is the movement of these smaller pieces. The same forces that break down rocks will often transport the smaller pieces to another location. These smaller pieces mix with sand, silt, and mud to become sediment.

Weathering and erosion chisel, polish, buff, chip, and carve Earth's surface to shape and reshape it every day. They are part of a process called the rock cycle.

## Did you Know?

**Plants roots are a major cause of weathering. When plants grow in cracks, it weakens the rock. As the plant grows, it further breaks down the rock.**

## The Rock Cycle

The rock cycle is the process through which rocks are broken down to create new ones. It begins when hot, liquid magma rises to the surface from Earth's mantle. At the surface, it cools and hardens, which creates igneous rocks. Over time, weathering breaks down these igneous rocks. Erosion carries the broken down pieces and mixes them with other matter like sand, silt, and mud. These become sediment, which settles into layers.

# What Are **EROSION AND WEATHERING?**

Crust

Mantle

Outer Core

Inner Core

Earth is made up of many layers. The top layer is the crust and is made of rock. Under the crust is a layer of magma called the mantle. Below the mantle is Earth's core, which is divided into two layers. The outer core is made up of melted metals, while the inner core is a ball of solid metal.

Eventually, these layers become sedimentary rocks. Metamorphic rock forms when heat and pressure change the sedimentary rocks. The rock cycle continues when events such as earthquakes push these rocks below the surface, where the hot magma melts them to create new rocks.

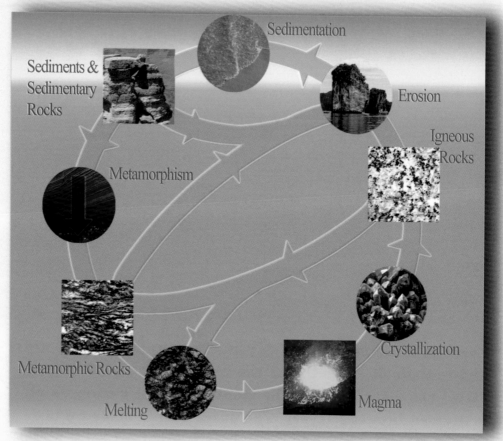

**The rock cycle is the process by which rocks are created.**

# Two Kinds of
# WEATHERING

There are two kinds of weathering: mechanical and chemical. They often occur at the same time.

**Coyote Gulch in Utah is an example of what happens over long periods of erosion and weathering.**

## Mechanical Weathering

A gentle breeze might not feel forceful to you. But wind blowing against a rock for a long time can break it down and physically change its shape. The wind scrapes off tiny pieces or it can blast rocks with sand and other small bits of matter. This is mechanical, or physical, weathering.

**Mechanical weathering occurs when forces like wind, water, and ice weaken a rock and break it down.**

Water can also physically weather rocks. When water flows over rocks, it can remove tiny pieces just like the wind can.

Water can also get trapped inside a rock. When the trapped water pushes against the rock to get out, it creates cracks in the rock.

Sometimes the water trapped inside a rock freezes. The ice expands and breaks off pieces of the rock.

# Two Kinds of **WEATHERING**

The holes in this sandstone rock formation in New Mexico were created by years of wind blowing against its surface.

## Did You Know?

Animals like moles can also cause mechanical weathering. When they tunnel through the earth, they help break down rocks.

**The force of waves crashing against rocks at the beach can cause the rock to break apart.**

## Chemical Weathering

Chemical weathering occurs when elements like oxygen cause substances in the rock to change by affecting its chemical makeup. These changes break apart the rock. Rust is an example of chemical weathering. Some rocks contain the mineral iron. When iron touches the oxygen in air, it rusts, which weakens the rock.

Acid rain can also cause weathering. The harsh chemicals in acid rain eat away at rocks.

Climate is another cause of chemical weathering. Rocks weather more quickly in hot, wet climates than they do in cool, dry ones. This is because the high temperatures and large amounts of water cause the rock's minerals to change.

# Two Kinds of **WEATHERING**

The buildup of rust during chemical
weathering turns rocks red.

## Did You Know?

Since 1998, Harvard University has
wrapped some of its bronze and
marble statues with waterproof
covers to protect them from acid
rain and snow.

# Causes of
# EROSION

Flowing water, blowing wind, and moving glaciers are powerful forces in the process of erosion.

## Washed Away by Water

After weathering has broken down rocks, erosion carries the bits of rock away. Erosion is the movement of particles, which can only happen after weathering has weakened them. A force like water takes the bits of rock downstream and mixes them with sand, silt, and mud to form sediment.

## Did You Know?

The Amazon River in South America deposits 3 million tons (2.7 million metric tons) of sediment in the ocean every day!

Water is key
to erosion's
transportation
process.

Erosion's transporting process begins with rainfall. When rain washes over a rock, the water not only weathers it, but it also carries away little pieces. The rain carrying the rock pieces flows into streams and rivers. Some of these flow into the ocean, where the matter settles into layers to create sediment.

## Blown Away by Wind

Wind is another driving force behind erosion. Wind can change the shape of rocks as it erodes their surface.

There are two kinds of wind erosion. Deflation happens when the wind picks up sand, silt, mud, and other matter. The heaver substances, such as bits of rock, stay behind as the wind carries away the lighter pieces of matter. This is how rocky deserts are created.

**This desert in Israel was created by deflation.**

# Causes of **EROSION**

Abrasion occurs when the wind carries away bits of sediment and blows them against a rock's surface. It sometimes forms tiny holes or scratches. Other times, it can polish a rock's surface until it is smooth and shiny. Sometimes, abrasion can carve huge holes into soil and rock. These holes are called blowouts.

**Blowouts are common on beaches and in deserts where there is a lot of wind.**

## Carved by Ice

In the North and South Poles, it is so cold that the snow never melts. Instead, the snow piles up until it is so thick and heavy that it turns into ice over time, which creates a glacier.

Glaciers move very slowly (only a few centimeters a day in some cases), but they are so hard and heavy that they erode everything in their path. Over thousands of years, a glacier can wear away huge rocks and even deposit them in another location hundreds of miles (kilometers) away. Sometimes, glaciers create valleys where mountains used to be.

**The Briksdal glacier in Norway scrapes Earth's surface as it moves.**

## Did You Know?

The Lambert Glacier in Antarctica is the largest glacier in the world. It is 270 miles (435 km) long, up to 60 miles (97 km) wide, and up to 8,200 feet (2,500 m) deep.

# Shaping and Reshaping EARTH'S SURFACE

Through wind, water, and ice, erosion is constantly changing Earth's surface by breaking down rocks and moving sediment around. This can create new landforms.

## Rock Formations

Wind can reshape Earth's surface and create some odd-looking formations. These occur because the wind cannot carry heavy sand more than six feet (two meters) above the ground. This sand carried by wind erodes just the bottom part of a rock. This creates rocks that look like giant mushrooms!

**This soil erosion in Ukraine was caused by water runoff.**

## Did You Know?

Caves are created by weathering and erosion! The Lost Sea in Sweetwater, Tennessee, is a cave that has an underground lake inside of it. The lake is home to a species of blind albino trout.

This rock on Balandra Beach in La Paz, Mexico, was formed by wind erosion.

## Deltas

Fast-moving water reshapes Earth by eroding rock to create canyons and valleys. When a river flows into an ocean, it can leave sediment behind. This sediment collects over time and creates new lands called deltas.

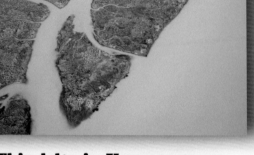

**This delta in Vancouver was created by eroded sediment.**

## Moraines

Glaciers also shape Earth's surface through erosion. As the climate gets warmer, glaciers melt and move, which leaves piles of sediment behind. These form hills called moraines.

Glaciers also carve valleys as they creep across Earth's surface and scrape at rocks.

**These frozen lakes and moraines are on the Ngozumpa Glacier in Nepal.**

## Did You Know?

Rising sea levels, caused by glaciers melting due to global warming, are causing islands to disappear! Tuvalu in the Pacific Ocean began evacuation of its 11,000 citizens in 2006. Scientists suggest that the Maldives in the Indian Ocean (shown here) will have to evacuate its 311,000 citizens in the next fifty years.

# Bad Effects of
# WEATHERING
# AND EROSION

Erosion is an important part of the rock cycle and has helped shape Earth's surface. However, its effects are not always good.

## Water Damage

When water moves in large amounts very quickly, it can cause a flash flood. These floods can wreck buildings and kill people.

**This strange rock formation is called Hvitserkur, and it is in Iceland.**

# Bad Effects of **WEATHERING AND EROSION**

**A flash flood can wash away everything
in its path in a very short time.**

Too much water can also cause sinkholes. Sinkholes form when water erodes underground rock. In time, there is not enough rock to support the surface and the surface collapses. This is especially dangerous on roadways.

**Water can erode the ground and cause roads to collapse.**

## Wind Damage

Wind can also cause damage through erosion. Blowing away topsoil can be especially harmful on farmland where crops are grown. People make erosion worse by cutting down trees or letting livestock like cows eat all the plants. Plants and their roots help hold the soil in place.

**Food cannot be grown on eroded land. Crops need rich topsoil to grow.**

## Landslides

Another dangerous side effect of weathering and erosion are landslides. Landslides occur when rocks, boulders, dirt, and pebbles collect on a hill or mountainside. When it rains or a harsh wind picks up, sometimes the weight pulls the mound down the hill. Landslides can be as small as a few pebbles or as large as an avalanche. Buildings and cars can be damaged, and people can be badly hurt. Landslides can block pathways.

**A landslide in Turkey buried buildings and cars under tons of earth and rock.**

# Why Are WEATHERING AND EROSION Important?

Although weathering and erosion can harm people and Earth by causing floods and soil erosion, these two processes are important. Weathering and erosion have shaped Earth's surface for millions of years. Without them, the rock cycle could not continue. Rocks would not be able to break down and form new rocks, and Earth's surface would never change.

Weathering and erosion take bits of rock and other matter to create sediment, which forms sedimentary rocks, as well as mountains, hills, deltas, and deserts. Life on Earth would be very different were it not for weathering and erosion.

Weathering and erosion can create all sorts of rock shapes.

# Glossary

**abrasion**—The rubbing together of rock and tiny bits of rock.

**deflation**—The movement of soil, sand, and dust by wind.

**delta**—A pile of earth and sand that collects at the mouth of a river.

**erosion**—The wearing away of land over time.

**glaciers**—Large masses of ice that move down a mountain or along a valley.

**igneous rocks**—Hot, liquid underground minerals that have cooled and hardened.

**metamorphic rock**—Rock that has been changed by heat and heavy weight.

**minerals**—Natural elements that are not animals, plants, or other living things.

**moraine**—A hill of earth and stones left behind by a glacier.

**sediment**—Gravel, sand, or mud carried by wind or water.

**sedimentary rocks**—Layers of stones, sand, or mud that have been pressed together to form rock.

**weathering**—The breaking up of rock by water, wind, and chemical forces.

# Further Reading

## BOOKS

Dee, Willa. *Erosion and Weathering (Rocks: the Hard Facts)*. New York: PowerKids Press, 2014.

Hoffman, Steven M. *Weathering and Erosion: Wearing Down Rocks (Rock It!)*. New York: PowerKids Press, 2011.

Nelson, Maria. *Weathering and Erosion (That Rocks!)*. New York: Gareth Stevens Publishing, 2013.

Riley, Joelle. *Examining Erosion*. New York: Lerner Publications, 2013

## WEBSITES

**One Geology Kids**

onegeology.org/extra/kids/earthProcesses/weathering.html

*Learn more about weathering and erosion in the rock cycle.*

**National Geographic**

science.nationalgeographic.com/science/earth/the-dynamic-earth/weathering-erosion-article/

*Official National Geographic website where you can discover details about weathering and erosion.*

**US Geological Survey**

geomaps.wr.usgs.gov/parks/misc/gweaero.html

*Official site of the United States Geological Survey. Discover the difference between weathering and erosion.*

# Index